CHINESE NEW YEAR

HOLIDAY CELEBRATIONS

Kieran Walsh

Rourke

Publishing LLC
Vero Beach, Florida 32964

www.rourkepublishing.com

PHOTO CREDITS: © Bob West pages 7, 13; © Associated Press all other photos.

Cover: *Children dressed in mouse costumes perform a dance at Bejing's Temple of the Earth.*

Editor: Frank Sloan

Cover Design by Nicola Stratford

Library of Congress Cataloging-in-Publication Data

Walsh, Kieran.
  Chinese New Year / Kieran Walsh.
    p. cm. — (Holiday celebrations)
Includes bibliographical references and index.
  ISBN 1-58952-215-X (hardcover)
  1. Chinese New Year. 2. Chinese New Year—United States. 3. United States—Social life and customs. I. Title. II. Holiday celebrations
(Vero Beach, Fla.)
  GT4905 .W27 2002
  394.261--dc21

                                        2002003666

Printed in the USA

CG/CG

TABLE OF CONTENTS

THE CHINESE CALENDAR

Chinese New Year takes place on a different date every year. This is because the Chinese follow a combined **lunar** calendar and **solar** calendar. A lunar calendar is based on cycles of the moon. A solar calendar is based on cycles of the sun. Although the date changes each year, Chinese New Year always begins in either January or February.

Children dress as tigers to celebrate the year of the Tiger.

THE YEAR OF THE HORSE

For the Chinese, 2002 is actually the year 4699. It is the year of the Horse. The Chinese calendar assigns every year to one of twelve signs. It is believed that a person's personality is determined by the sign of the year in which they were born. The other eleven signs include the Rat, Ox, Tiger, Rabbit, Dragon, Snake, Sheep, Monkey, Bird, Dog, and Boar.

Paradegoers celebrate the year of the Horse in San Francisco.

THE CELEBRATION

The celebration of Chinese New Year lasts fifteen days. It begins with the first of the holiday and ends with the Lantern Festival. Many American cities like New York, San Francisco, and Philadelphia have areas with a large Chinese population. These places are known as Chinatown. For the fifteen days of Chinese New Year, Chinatown comes alive with fireworks, music, and parades.

Children take part in the lion dance in New York's Chinatown.

HOW IT BEGAN

The Chinese word **Nian** means "year." Legend has it that the Nian was the name of a monster that terrified the people of a small Chinese village every year on New Year's Eve. In order to scare away the Nian, people began shooting firecrackers, waving red banners, and pounding on drums and gongs. The Nian was chased away, and the people of the village celebrated their victory.

Noise and smoke from firecrackers are used to scare away legendary monsters.

A young girl lights a joss stick to pray for good luck.

Fancy decorations take months to prepare.

THE START OF SPRING

Chinese New Year is a happy time because it is considered to be the end of winter and the beginning of spring. Chinese New Year is sometimes called the Spring Festival.

Also, the Chinese mark their age according to the New Year. The seventh day of the Chinese New Year is called **Yan Yat**, meaning everybody's birthday.

Colorful costumes and lanterns brighten a parade float.

GETTING READY

Preparations for Chinese New Year begin about a month before. People shop for presents, food, clothing, and decorations. Chinese families clean their homes. This is done to get rid of any bad luck the family may have had over the year. People decorate with special poems that wish happiness, wealth, and long lives.

Releasing a caged bird is thought to give a person good luck.

NEW YEAR'S EVE AND NEW YEAR'S DAY

On New Year's Eve, Chinese families have a special feast of seafood and dumplings. Dessert is always **Nian Gao** – a special New Year's Cake. Everyone stays up late to watch the midnight fireworks.

On New Year's Day families go door to door to visit. They exchange gifts with their relatives and neighbors. It is thought to be bad luck to fight or argue at the start of a New Year. Everyone is warm and friendly toward each other.

Fireworks light the night sky during a New Year celebration in Hong Kong.

THE LANTERN FESTIVAL

The tradition of the Lantern Festival dates back to when people believed that spirits flew through the night sky. During the Lantern Festival colorful lanterns of every size and shape are displayed.

A special treat is the lion dance. Enormous lions with flashing eyes parade through the streets accompanied by drums and cymbals. Sometimes the figures used are dragons.

A man helps his friends put on their lion costumes at the start of the parade.

GETTING READY FOR NEXT YEAR

With the Lantern Festival, Chinese New Year comes to an end and normal life resumes. However, everyone is happy after celebrating Chinese New Year. People return to their jobs and daily lives with a new sense of family and goodwill. Plus, they have a chance to rest before next year's celebration!

GLOSSARY

lunar (LOON uhr) — something based on cycles of the moon

Nian (nee UHN) — a Chinese word that means "year"

Nian Gao (nee UHN GO) — a special Chinese New Year's dessert

solar (SOH luhr) — something based on cycles of the sun

Yan Yat (YAHN YAHT) — the seventh day of Chinese New Year

INDEX

Further Reading

Hoyt-Goldsmith, Diane. *Celebrating Chinese New Year*. Holiday House, 1998
Marx, David. *Chinese New Year*. Children's Press, 2002
Robinson, Fay. *Chinese New Year*. Enslow, 2001

Websites To Visit

http://chineseculture.about.com/cs/newyear/index.htm
http://www.chinapage.com/newyear.html
http://www.kiddyhouse.com/CNY/

About The Author

Kieran Walsh is a writer of children's nonfiction books, primarily on historical and social studies topics. A graduate of Manhattan College, in Riverdale, NY, his degree is in Communications. Walsh has been involved in the children's book field as editor, proofreader, and illustrator as well as author.